The Little
Book of
Kaizen

For Henry and James Jazz: may things continue to get better every single day

The Little
Book of
Kaizen

The Japanese art of
transformation, one
small step at a time

Suzannah Lee

Contents

A Perfect Life
Introduction to Kaizen 6

Five, Four, Three, Two, One
Mindfulness, Meditation and Making
Things Happen 18

For Want of a Nail
Kaizen and the Five-Why System 32

From Tiny Acorns…
Point Kaizen 49

…Mighty Oaks Grow
System Kaizen 59

The Best It Can Be
Kaizen and the Five-S System 79

A Perfect Life

Introduction to Kaizen

Picture your perfect life.

No, not that: picture your life, perfected. Picture your life through an Instagram filter; picture your life in a Pinterest folder. Picture your life as it is now, but *polished*: all those annoying loose ends tied up in a bow, every part moving smoothly, the whole a well-oiled machine. Picture your life with all the kinks ironed out, everything easy, everything tidy, everything good. Picture your perfect life.

Picture, maybe, ironed bedding and tights that never have a hole in; picture going for a run every morning and *enjoying* it; picture daintily snacking on a handful of almonds as you finish a bit of work, on time, on deadline, at your clear desk.

Picture four colours of Post-its, always knowing exactly where your keys are, and a kitchen full of Kilner jars neatly labelled in pastel chalk paint. Or your equivalent. Maybe you hate Kilner jars and never cook. Maybe running and almonds don't feature for you. Maybe you never wear tights. It doesn't matter. These just happen to be mine. And your perfect life won't be mine, and mine won't be yours – but our paths to that end might just be the same.

You've come to this book, I think, because you feel other people have that kind of life, and you don't, and there's a part of you that's still wondering why you can't. There's a part of you — a tiny, hopeful part of you — that wonders if you *could*. That tiny, hopeful part there? That's the point of this book.

This book is about nourishing that tiny, hopeful heart of yours; about blowing on the spark of that desire to be better and kindling it into a roaring, gorgeous flame. Why *shouldn't* you have a life where everything works? Why *shouldn't* you have the kind of world you've always wanted?

Let's steer clear of words like 'deserve', because things happen to people all the time that they don't deserve: the world is full of good things happening to bad people and vice versa. Let's stick instead to this: you can make your life better. You can make it better right now.

This is a book about the now, and how it can change your future; how the next five minutes can change the next hour and the next hour can change the next day.

This is a book about accepting where we are and working from there. This is a book about not chucking in your whole diet because you really fancied some chips; about starting small; about starting from where you are, not where you wish you might be.

This is a manual for living your life the way you want to live your life, starting right now. This is a guide to living in the moment with one eye on what's coming round the corner.

It's about starting now, not later; it's about not putting off until tomorrow what you could do today; it's about a stitch in time saving nine. It's about having more time. It's about small, manageable, achievable goals that somehow stack up to make a huge difference.

It's about how little things make the big things happen. It's about baby steps. One small step for man, one giant leap for mankind. It's about becoming who you want to be in a way that works for you. Oh, and it's about a Japanese philosophy of business efficiency. It's about *kaizen*.

Kaizen

/kʌɪˈzɛn/   *noun*

Japanese,

lit. 'a change for the better', '(an) improvement',
< *kai* revision, change + *zen* (the) good.

A Japanese business philosophy, most famously
implemented in the Toyota factories, of continuous
improvement in working practices, personal
efficiency, etc.; hence, an improvement in
performance or productivity.

Oxford English Dictionary

Kaizen in real life

How can a business philosophy of improvement, most famously implemented for increased efficiency in the Toyota factories, apply to you, at home or on the bus to work or dropping the kids off at school? How can this be something that will change *your* life?

Look: there's a certain face that most people make when you tell them you're working on a book about Japanese business efficiency. I imagine it's quite similar to the face you're making now (if you didn't realize this was a book about Japanese business efficiency but have turned to this page anyway). It's a sort of *inadequate* face: as if they feel like they won't be good enough for the minimal, elegant life you're about to tell them to lead; as if they are pretty sure you're about to judge them for the number of odd socks secretly shoved in the back of a drawer or the chaos of their email inbox. It's like they (and maybe you, too!) assume we're after a kind of unattainable, instant perfection — and *that's just not true.* I promise you.

We're after perfection, sure. Why not? But it's perfection that's within reach. It's a new kind of perfection: one that changes with you, one that grows with you, one that *begins* with you. I promise you: you are good enough for this book.

You are good enough to make your life better. You've heard of Marie Kondo; now level up to kaizen. What Kondo can do for your home, your possessions and your wardrobe, kaizen can do for your life.

Remember that Marie Kondo doesn't want you, necessarily, to throw everything away and live in immaculate monochrome: she simply wants you to consider whether *you* do. Is the way you're living bringing you happiness? Are the things in your life 'sparking joy'? Is everything in your home there for a purpose?

In this book, we're going to apply that philosophy, pretty much, to everything you do – from the minute you get up in the morning to the moment you fall asleep at night. And, if we're being honest, probably the sleep you're getting, too. Is this as good as it could be? Is everything in my life as good as it could be? Am I living my best life?

If this feels daunting, keep reading. The whole point of kaizen is to change things little by little: to make every day a little better than the last. It's about the freedom to make changes where you need to make changes; and to be open to that change whenever and wherever you see it.

The word kaizen is often translated as 'continuous improvement', although it literally just means 'improvement': 'good change'. Remember those faces that people make when you say 'Japanese business efficiency'? It's this kind of thing that's the problem: this urge to complicate things in translation that are actually very simple.

Kaizen isn't a complex system – not at heart. It's just about looking at your life properly and regularly to make sure it's doing what you want it to be doing. If it is, fantastic. If it isn't, fix it.

Kaizen simply gives us the tools to see what we're doing, why we're doing it, and whether we're going where we want to go. This book is not an authoritative guide on running a hyper-efficient car factory. It's simply using the tips and tricks of a highly successful system to make you into a highly successful person. Whatever that success might look like to you.

The five steps of kaizen

The ideal kaizen approach is widely regarded as having five steps: *standardize, measure, compare, innovate, standardize.* This doesn't exactly feel promising for domestic application, does it? This feels very much like a business–efficiency mechanism. But all through this book, that's what we'll be doing. We might not use these crisp, technical names – but that's what's going on.

This isn't a book about kaizen as it's practised in the Toyota factory: this is a book informed by a kaizen approach to life, as this book can inform your life. These five steps are integral to everything we'll be doing here. Five is sometimes considered a lucky number in Japan, perhaps because of the five elements (earth, water, wind, fire and the void). That's why there are five chapters in this book (plus this introduction and a conclusion: we cheated a bit). Five for the five steps of kaizen; five for the five of five-why; five for the five of five-S.

We'll run through a series of exercises, thought experiments and tasks, each designed to help us move forward to the kind of life we want all-round. We're going to take control of our uncontrollable lives; we're going to make (ourselves, practically, tangibly, genuinely) the kind of world we want to see. There's a lot of questions in this book: far more questions than there are answers. But that's because kaizen as a system is all about looking at the truth, and whether the truth is as good as it could be. It's all about taking control of your own answers, yourself. Kaizen is control; kaizen is change; kaizen is the hope of something being better, day after day.

And yes, I know. All this is a lot. So let's start with something a bit easier.

Let's just count, very simply, to — what else? — five.

1

Five, Four, Three, Two, One

Mindfulness, Meditation and Making Things Happen

The first exercise in this book is a centring and grounding one. It's designed to pull you into the moment, and anchor you in the here-and-now. It will take you perhaps a minute, with no equipment, and no need to move. (We'll come back to this exercise again and again, so give it a whirl now and then you've got it in the bag for later.)

There is something essentially calming about this kind of exercise: small, domestic and perhaps a little bit silly, true. But calming, nonetheless. We're going to use it, in this book, as a kind of mental re-set; a regular check-in with ourselves and with our world, and as a jumping-off point for the kind of self-analysis that makes kaizen so successful.

5-4-3-2-1

This exercise is incredibly simple, and it starts with a sit-down. Or a lie-down. Or even a stand. Get comfortable: as comfortable as you can, exactly where you are. Roll your shoulders back, and breathe in. Breathe deeply.

You're going to breathe in through the nose for a count of five; hold for a count of five; and out through the mouth for a count of five. In (2, 3, 4, 5) and hold (2, 3, 4, 5) and out (2, 3, 4, 5).

Do this five times, and as you do it feel the air coming in to your lungs, right down to the bottom of your ribcage: notice whether the air is warm, or whether it's cold; notice how it feels when it expands your ribs, and the gentle sound it makes as it leaves your lips. In, hold, out. In, hold, out.

Don't rush it; don't hurry it. Just keep breathing. In, hold, out.

Now, keeping your breathing steady, try to notice
the following, one at a time:

FIVE things you can see

FOUR things you can hear

THREE things you can touch

TWO things you can smell

ONE thing you can taste

Slowly notice; slowly breathe; feel the air filling
and emptying your body as you exist in the world.
You exist; that's all you have to do for this exercise.
That's the only place we can possibly begin: existing,
just as we are, in the here and now.

Kaizen and the art of mindfulness

What we just did in the exercise on the previous pages is taken from the practise of mindfulness: the art of learning to notice where you are, and when you are. Now, look. I know that over the last few years it's been hard to escape 'mindfulness'. It's become a bit of a trend – and a bit of a buzzword for a particular kind of smug Instagram influencer. But it's so much more than that. For unlike other hipster faves like rose gold or terrariums, mindfulness has a very real, tangible therapeutic impact.

(If you want to be mindful among your terrariums and rose-gold kitchen bits, that's also pretty great. If rose gold and succulents make you happy, that's what this book is all about.)

'Paying more attention to the present moment – to your own thoughts and feelings, and to the world around you – can improve your mental wellbeing,' say the NHS guidelines – and it's hard to argue. Recommended by the National Institute for Health and Care Excellence (NICE) as a preventative for depression, it's widely recognized that a mindful approach to life can *change* your life. Not only that, there's significant evidence to suggest that it might help physical health, too. (A Harvard study of 2018[1] found that this kind of mindful meditation could reduce blood pressure, and even alter your genetic responses for the better.)

But what's all this got to do with kaizen? Why are we taking so long to get to the kaizen part? This isn't *The Little Book of Mindfulness*, after all. But here's the thing: it's all connected. How can we change our lives if we don't know what our lives are? How can we see where we're going wrong if we don't see clearly?

[1] www.ncbi.nlm.nih.gov/pubmed/29616846

Write it down

Remember those five steps? *Standardize, measure, compare, innovate, standardize?* We can't begin to standardize – and don't worry, I promise, we're going to get to each bit in time – until we have an idea of what we're standardizing. This isn't the Toyota factory. We're not trying to produce a hundred identical cars. We're trying to produce a single individual life, tailor-made for the person producing it.

We're trying to make something unique – and that means I can't just tell you where to start. You have to decide it for yourself, and that means taking some time to get to know yourself. It means mindfulness. It means meditation. It means taking these five minutes (first, just today, but, in time, every day) for yourself, to look at your life, and to look at what you want from it.

Over the course of this book, we're going to write some things down. There's some space provided on these pages – but this is, of course, a 'little book' and space is at a bit of a premium round here.

If you can, you're going to find it helpful to have a new notebook and a couple of colours of pen. A really nice notebook. Your favourite pen. Yes, a cheap biro and the back of an envelope would do – but where's the fun in that?

And sure, there's nothing magic or more efficient about stationery – but there's something special about knowing you've got exactly the right tools for the job. This is a book about living the life you want, remember. This is a book about doing things the way you've always wanted to. Pick out a notebook that makes you feel like the best version of yourself. Pick out a pen in a colour that makes you happy.

Writing things down has been scientifically proven to help with stress and anxiety – and in some cases, even severe mental-health problems like PTSD. Writing out our feelings, anxieties, hopes and fears puts them into words – and nothing is more unsettling than the unknown. How can we tackle our fears if we don't know what they are? How can we make a map if we don't know where we want to go?

So, let's write.

We're going to write things down for a few reasons:

to create a record of where we are

to create a plan for where we want to go

to measure where we're really going

to see how these three things compare with each other

to make a space that belongs just to ourselves.

The first four are obviously kaizen in practice, sure – but that last one is a bit of a curve ball.

Carving out a space that's just ours (just mine, just yours) can be difficult. It's hard to make time for who we are apart from the demands of work and family and the world – and the person all those people need us to be.

We've said that the function of this chapter is to see more clearly, and we need to start by seeing ourselves as we truly are, and we can't do that without some space. We can't do that without opening a fresh new workbook that's just for us, and nobody else. Not for work notes. Not for the kids to scribble in. Not for tearing a page out. Just for you. This space is just for you. Remember that cliché about fastening your own oxygen mask before attending to the needs of others? This is your oxygen mask.

And in that same vein, this book needs you to make a little time for yourself: say, half an hour, in a quiet place. If this feels impossible, I get it. I do. But this is crucial. Feel guilty about taking that half-hour away from your work or your kids or your jobs? Don't.

This is the first step to making all and any of those things better. This is the first step to you being the best worker, the best parent, the best version of you that you can be.

General Wellbeing

Let's go back to the breathing we practised earlier (see page 20); five in, five hold, five out. We're going to notice the 5–4–3–2–1 of the senses all around us. This is the grounding part of the exercise, to bring us into our own bodies and the real world. You're good at this; you've done it before.

I want you to ask yourself the following questions. They aren't easy questions, and this won't necessarily be easy. Be honest; be clear. Try to resist the temptation to smooth over any bad feelings, hard feelings or complications. Don't sugar-coat it: this is a starting-point, just for you. Read the question, take a moment to focus with the breathing exercise, and jot down a few notes.

How am I, in myself, physically?

How am I, in myself, mentally?

Then try:

Why did I pick up this book?

Why am I doing this exercise?

While these questions may sound facetious, they are actually very serious. People don't turn to self-help books when everything is perfect. People don't pick up books like this unless they want something to change. Chances are, you picked up this book because something is *wrong*.

Something isn't working the way you want it to. So what is it?

What's not working for you?

What isn't making you happy? What's taking you away from your best life?

(Maybe you don't know. Maybe it's *everything*. And that's fine, too. Whatever brought you here, you're welcome, and you're ready, and we're going to make it better.)

2

For Want
of a Nail

Kaizen and the
Five-Why System

The thing about kaizen is that it's about change, sure — but efficient change. It's about changing the right thing, at the right time, for the right reasons. There's no point blundering in and trying to make everything different immediately, now, yesterday: that only leads to more chaos. We need to know what we're doing and why we're doing it. We need to know why something isn't working before we know how to change it.

There's no point planning to write better apology emails for your lateness if you could simply . . . stop being late; there's no point working out the quickest route to the vending machine if you could simply put a snack in your bag the night before; there's no point building a beautiful Wallace-and-Gromit-esque machine to whisk your toast out before it burns if you could simply turn the toaster down before you put the bread in. A failure to see the root causes of things means that we're going to keep making the same mistakes, over and over again.

We need to find out why things go wrong to stop them going wrong in future, and it's for that reason that one of the most crucial steps of kaizen is a tool called the 'five-why' system. It's called the 'five-why' system because asking 'why' five times is believed to be enough to get you to the root cause of the problem – and that's the thing you should really be tackling.

For Want of a Nail

Remember the old rhyme?

For want of a nail, the shoe was lost;

For want of a shoe, the horse was lost;

For want of a horse, the rider was lost;

For want of a rider, the battle was lost;

For want of a battle, the kingdom was lost;

And all for the want of a horseshoe nail.

A five-why approach to this loss of a kingdom might look like this:

Why did we lose the kingdom?
Because we lost the battle.

Why did we lose the battle?
Because we lost the rider.

Why did we lose the rider?
Because we lost the horse.

Why did we lose the horse?
Because we lost the shoe.

Why did we lose the shoe?
Because we lost the nail.

The theory of 'five why' is that we should be asking ourselves these kind of interrogative five-step questions for everything that goes wrong in our lives.

In this chapter, we're going to talk through a hypothetical situation, in order to demonstrate both the technique and value of the 'five-why' system. You'll need your notebook now – and to think of a situation that didn't work for you in the way you wanted it to. Each time we interrogate the hypothetical situation, I want you to follow suit for your own real life: this way, you'll embed the technique into your mind, and have it to hand next time you need it.

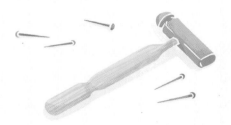

Applying the five-why system

Take, for instance, the very tedious problem of having to pay a small fine for late payment of taxes. This is a fairly minor, irritating problem – in the grand scheme of things. Let's take that, and run it through the system practised above:

1. Why did you have to pay a fine?
Because you were late filing your taxes.

2. Why were you late filing your taxes?
Because you couldn't find your credit card to pay them.

3. Why couldn't you find your credit card?
Because you didn't put it somewhere safe.

4. Why didn't you put it somewhere safe?
Because you didn't have somewhere safe to put it.

5. Why didn't you have somewhere safe to put it?
…

And to the last one, of course, there's an obvious solution: find somewhere safe to keep your credit card. Get a wallet. Put the card in the wallet every time.

It isn't the solution you might have come to without the five-why: the answer isn't just 'pay the fine' or even 'pay your taxes on time'. There's a structural problem in your life – in this instance, not having somewhere safe to put your credit card – and that structural problem is almost certainly going to have affected other things, too. The tax fine won't be the only boring, small, joy-sucking problem that misplacing your credit card could cause; and by solving that structural problem right now, you've got ahead of the game.

It's often recommended to plot these five-why answers in what's called an '*ishikawa*', or 'fishbone', diagram, like this:

Effect

Problem

Take your notebook – the one we started in the previous chapter. Start on the left of the page, with the problem. Draw a line across the page (the 'spine' of the fishbone, if you will) and from that spine/line, draw a series of smaller lines. Each one of these smaller lines represents something that led to the problem. You'll see in this diagram there's more than one 'rib-bone' coming off the 'spine'. That's because – having asked ourselves the five-whys once, we're now going to do it again. We're going to do it five times.

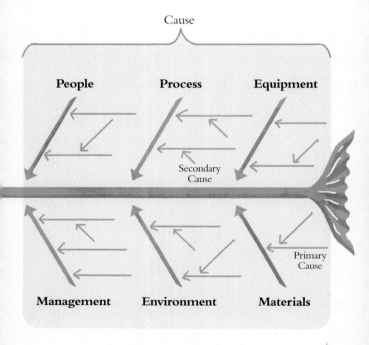

Five times, because there's often not just one cause of a problem. We're going to identify five different things you could have done differently, and ask 'why' each time. Let's look at our tax-fine example again:

1. Why did you have to pay a fine?
Because you were late filing your taxes.

2. Why were you late filing your taxes?
Because you waited until the last day to do it, and then a small problem (the lost credit card) held you up.

3. Why did you wait until the last day to do it?
Because you were doing other work.

4. Why were you doing other work?
Because you took on too much work.

5. Why did you take on too much work?
...

And just like that, we've identified another root cause: a bigger one this time, one that you really need to think about. One that, perhaps, has an emotional answer instead of a practical one.

Hansei

Like all of kaizen, this is unbelievably simple in theory
– but when you're using it to assess your whole life instead
of the efficiency of a car manufacturer, it can get fairly
sticky fairly quickly. It can take us into places that are dark,
and hard, and make us feel guilty and weird – because
feelings are more complicated than factories. But none of
that means we shouldn't do it. Actually, it means it's more
necessary than ever.

There is a concept in Japanese culture which we don't really
have in the West, known as 'hansei'. 'Hansei' means 'self-
reflection' – as in, the idea that self-reflection is crucial to
self-improvement, and that self-improvement is crucial to us
all. What it amounts to practically is a sense that we need to
take responsibility for ourselves, and for our own mistakes:
the first thing we should look to when something goes
wrong is our own behaviour. We shouldn't seek to blame
others before we've worked out how much blame to place
at our own door.

Put like this, of course, it's clear that it's part of every culture – think of the Bible's exhortation to 'take out the plank in your own eye before attending to the speck in your brother's' – but can feel rather overwhelming when placed in the spotlight.

Try not to be overwhelmed – and try not to feel guilty. Guilt isn't going to help us move forward; and guilt isn't going to help us deal with the feelings that are causing us problems.

Are You Sure?

To live kaizen, we need to apply five-why to everything in our lives – to our practical actions, and our emotional wellbeing, too. There's a technique in some therapeutic practices called the 'Are You Sure?' game, and the 'five-why' system is simply a formalized extension of that. In the 'Are You Sure?' game we identify a feeling – especially one that seems rootless or out of control.

The 'Are You Sure?' game goes like this:

I'm angry.

Why?
Because she ate my apple pie.

Are you sure?
OK, because she always eats my pie.

Are you sure?

You say a statement; you ask why; and then you ask: *are you sure?* Are you sure *that's* why? Is that really the reason? Is that the only reason? Is it more complicated?

Like this:

> *I'm angry.*
>
> Why?
> *Because she ate my apple pie.*
>
> Are you sure?
> *OK, because she always eats my pie.*
>
> Are you sure?
> *OK, because she often takes things that belong to me.*

Think of how a therapist will let the patient do the talking:
in this case, you're both therapist and patient, and you need
to ask yourself these small interrogative questions. It's easy to
see how something simple as 'she ate my apple
pie' can really have deeper, underlying
roots — maybe you need to set
better boundaries. Maybe she
needs a therapist of her own.

The natural next step of the 'Are You Sure?' game is to blur it into the five-why system. It's about cause and effect. Something happened – why? Why did that happen? Why? Why? Why?

I'm angry.

Why?
Because she ate my apple pie.

Are you sure?
OK, because she always eats my pie.

Are you sure?
OK, because she often takes things that belong to me.

Why?
Because I don't set clear boundaries.

Why?
Because I want people to like me.

Why?
Because I worry people don't like me . . .

And then, you see, you can start to tackle the real problem – just as with the lost credit card or the missing horseshoe nail.

Getting to these deep emotional truths is at the core of what kaizen can bring to us from a wellness perspective. If we know why we're having certain feelings, it's easier to keep them in check; if we know why we're behaving in certain unproductive ways, it's easier to channel those feelings into something that helps rather than hinders.

We've said that a failure to see the root causes of things means that we're going to keep making the same mistakes over and over again: if we apply this logic to our personal wellbeing, it's obvious that making the same emotional mistakes over and over again could have a dramatic impact on our happiness and ability to thrive.

3

From Tiny Acorns...

Point Kaizen

Point kaizen

There are two main approaches to kaizen: *system kaizen* and *point kaizen*. We're going to look at both, as they go hand in hand. By itself, each approach is fine: together, they can change your life. This is why kaizen is so effective: essentially, point kaizen is about the moment in which we're existing, and system kaizen is about the life we're living.

For effective change, you need to be grounded in the moment and to have an idea of where you're going. You need to be able to solve the small problems (nowhere to put the credit card!) and the big problems (emotional truths!).

We'll start with point kaizen, because point kaizen is so easy to write about that it feels mildly fraudulent even to put into a book. You can sum it up in three words, so simple a child could understand; you can start doing it right now, with no equipment or training or money or time. Those three words? *Do the thing.*

Do the thing. It's broken? Fix it. It's dirty? Clean it. It's in the wrong place? Put it in the right place. Do the thing. Do it now, not tomorrow, not the next day. Don't do it in five minutes, do it now. Point kaizen is everyone's mother. Point kaizen is the enemy of procrastination, and the successful practice of point kaizen – or whatever you want to call this kind of get-on-with-it attitude – is the single biggest difference between people who live that perfect life, and people who don't.

And here's the thing: you know that. You already know that point kaizen works. So why don't you do it? Why don't I do it? What's stopping us? In this book – in the next chapter – we're going to explore these reasons; and put in place a series of strategies, exercises, mantras and tips to help us successfully implement point kaizen in our lives.

It's hard to believe that something so obvious and simple could change lives – but without point kaizen, system kaizen is nothing. From tiny acorns, huge oak trees grow; and from efficient moments, perfect lives are formed.

This, to me, seems like the most pragmatic part of kaizen. We're going to look around and do something that makes the world – our world – better. And we're going to do it now.

The following three exercises are very simple – but it's their simplicity that makes them so effective. Life is complicated enough. Let's not overthink this. Let's just – in true kaizen style – get the thing done.

We're not going to think past the task that needs doing (not yet, anyway). We're not going to worry about why or what or how. We're just going to *do the thing*.

The Five-minute Fix

This exercise is based on a very simple concept: you can do anything for a minute, and you can do most things for five minutes. It comes from a time-management conceit called the *pomodoro technique*, developed in the 1980s by Italian student Francesco Cirillo. It takes its name from the tomato timer used by Cirillo — but any timer will work fine.

It's literally this: you are going to *do the thing* for five minutes. Clean your room for five minutes. Write for five minutes. Stretch for five minutes. You are going to do nothing else — not read this, nothing — until you've accomplished that five-minute goal.

Choose your five-minute target. Five breaths in, five breaths out, just as we practised (see page 20). Focus your mind on the immediate task ahead. Nothing else. Nothing more. Just the next five minutes.

Set a timer — tomato or otherwise. Now go. Get it done. See you back here in five.

The Five-thing Fix

Five breaths in, five breaths out, as always (see page 20). Look around you.

Find five tasks, each of which can be accomplished in under a minute: five problems with immediate solutions. Maybe they are to do with you physically; maybe mentally; maybe your environment. Maybe other things, too.

Here's my list:

- Empty coffee cup on the table

- Back hurts from sitting too long

- Wastepaper basket overflowing

- Iron and ironing board left out

- Urgent email needs quick response

And here's my list of solutions:

- Coffee cup in dishwasher
- Stretch!
- Empty the bin
- Put the iron away
- Reply to the email

See? It's that laughably simple. Five problems. Five solutions. Five things that can be accomplished in five minutes, and five things that you won't have to worry about for the rest of the day.

Do it. Do the things. Get them done.

The Five-step Fix

Five breaths in, five breaths out, as always (see page 20).

Remember the horrible exercise on pages 30–31? The one where we thought about all the reasons we'd come to this book for help in the first place? Pick one. Write it down on a clean page of your notebook and put a circle around it.

Right now, without thinking too much about it, write down five things that might improve it.

Now, for each of those, think of five things that might help you achieve each of those things.

Can any of these last twenty-five things be accomplished now, in the next five minutes? Can you take steps towards any of them right now? If so, do it. Don't read any further. Do it.

Congratulations: you're now making concrete steps towards solving your problems. You're just a few steps closer to a better life.

The simplicity of these exercises means you can immediately incorporate them into your ordinary day. Do a five-minute fix once in the morning and once in the afternoon. Do a five-thing fix once an hour, or every couple of hours. Do a five-step fix once a week, checking in with yourself every time to see what's helping. And be proud of yourself for doing it.

These are such small wins, but they are still wins. They are goals you have achieved, and we need to celebrate and acknowledge small goals. We're looking for a better life here – a happier and more fulfilling life – and these little hits of dopamine we get from meeting small goals are exactly what the doctor ordered. Don't you immediately feel better?

Taking things further

But, of course, not everything can be solved in five minutes – point kaizen (perhaps the most immediately useful implement in our kaizen toolbox) can sometimes act as a mask for more complex problems. It might be that the solution to, say, backache is to take that five minutes every hour to stretch – but it might be that you need to change your desk set-up. It might even be that you can't spend so long at your computer any more. It might be that you should see your doctor, or a physio.

Think back to our example in the previous chapter. It's easy to see that a point-kaizen approach might not fit very well with a five-why approach to finding a solution:

Problem: She ate my apple pie!
Solution: *Hide the pie!*

and might in fact stop us from addressing the real issues that lie beneath. It's important, then, to give ourselves time on a regular basis to assess what kind of problem we're dealing with – and what kind of approach to take. Is it a one-off? Is it something more complex? Is it both? Let's turn to the next chapter to consider the bigger picture.

4

... Mighty Oaks Grow

System Kaizen

System kaizen

If the last chapter was about the next five minutes, this chapter is about how the next five minutes can shape the next fifty years.

These are the mighty oaks that grow from those tiny acorns – so we need to be sure that we're planting the right acorns in the right place. There's no point making choices in the next five minutes that aren't helping us. There's even less point making choices that are going to actively hinder us.

This might sound terrifying, but what it really means is that we've always got the opportunity to do better: it's never too late to change. We've always got the power, in the next five minutes, to take small steps that will make a giant leap for our futures.

You don't have to start smoking a pack a day again just because you had a cigarette yesterday: all you have to do is not have a cigarette in the next five minutes. Your diet isn't over because you caved and ate a biscuit: all you have to do is not eat a biscuit in the next five minutes. Because the house is a mess now, it doesn't mean you're going to live in chaos for ever: you've got the next five minutes to make a real difference.

You get the idea. But if point kaizen is about doing the thing — about starting now, wherever and whenever you are — system kaizen is about knowing why we're doing it.

Where do you want to go?

So we've grounded ourselves thoroughly in the moment. We looked at who and where we are right now. We fixed the things that are troubling us right now. Now it's time to look at the bigger picture. It's time to look at where we want to go.

System kaizen is about overhauling the whole damn machine: you do it bit by bit, over a long time, refining and fixing things that you didn't even realize when you started were inefficient or inept or just plain wrong. The clue is in the name: it's systematic change.

System kaizen is about implementing kaizen, and the ideas of kaizen, into your life for ever. It's having your notebook. It's buying this book, and not just skimming it once, but practising it over and over again. It's about doing the breathing exercises and five-minute fixes and five-thing fixes and five-why assessments as a matter of course; and about making time for yourself to assess every element of your life as a matter of course, too.

It's about taking nothing for granted, and about knowing that everything can always be just a little bit better. It's about making sure that every moment – every fragment of our day – is a building block towards our perfect life. An efficient life is one that leaves the most time, after all, for joy.

EXERCISE:

A Day, a Week, a Life

Take your notebook. Without thinking too hard about it, jot down the elements that comprise a typical day. Not your best day, not your worst. Just an ordinary day, where you do averagely well at things. Average exercise, average diet. Be as honest as you can. Use the timetable opposite as a framework. If it helps, imagine you're a celebrity being interviewed for one of those features on the last page of a glossy magazine.

What time do you get up? When do you go to bed? How long do you spend getting dressed? How long do you spend actually working, and how much time do you spend staring into space? (You know you spend some time staring into space.) Now keep the timetable with you for a week and make sure it's accurate. (You will almost certainly find you spend much more time staring into space than you thought you did.)

Do you do the same thing every day? How much variation is there? This timetable should be as typical as possible: again, not your best day, not your worst. Don't worry about changing anything just yet. (Remember those five pillars of kaizen? What we're looking at here is *standardizing*. I told you you wouldn't even notice.)

6AM	3PM
7AM	4PM
8AM	5PM
9AM	6PM
10AM	7PM
11AM	8PM
NOON	9PM
1PM	10PM
2PM	11PM

After a week, we're going to look at this timetable again. We'll come back to it later in the chapter. Hang on.

Kaikaku

System kaizen, as an approach, is often complemented by an opposite approach called *kaikaku*. Kaikaku is about radical change: about changing the whole direction of a company, or — in our case — a life.

This may well be scary. I know this may well be scary, and I'm certainly not going to advocate we do that right now. We're grown-ups. We can't just drop everything and change everything — and that's absolutely not what this book promised. But just as we used meditation and mindfulness to shine a light on certain elements of this approach in the previous chapter, we're going to use kaikaku here. We're going to pretend radical change is possible. We're going to pretend — just for now, in the safety of this chapter in the cosy middle of the book — that anything is possible.

For the next exercise, you're going to need your notebook again: your notebook and a bit of time — and a bit of imagination.

I Dreamed a Dream . . .

Take your notebook, and breathe as we practised on page 20. This time, though, I want you to focus on one question to begin with.

What did you want to be when you were a kid?

Really focus on what you wanted to be when you grew up; really focus on what Little You thought your life might look like. Ballerina? Astronaut? Doctor? Parent? Professor? Painter? Witch? Puppy?

Imagine as many elements of this as you can: what did you think you would wear? Where did you think you would live? What did you hope for?

Be silly with this exercise; have fun with it. Play with it — and trust that nobody but you will see your writing here!

Use this space to dream like you did when you were a little kid: draw a picture, scribble labels on it, or anything that comes into your head. Maybe you wanted to be more than one thing at once: the first ballerina–firefighter–puppy in space. Anything was possible then. (And just maybe, things are still possible now…)

Look at everything you've written, and perhaps the things you've drawn, too. Here's the second question:

Why did you want this when you were a child?

Remember the five-why system? Bring that in here, too. Really interrogate what you wanted then. If you don't remember, work through it logically. Did you want to help people? To feel free? Did you want to build order out of chaos, or make something beautiful?

What we're building is a list of values: things that mattered to our younger selves. Play with this, too: word-clouds, little doodles, it all helps. If you aren't sure, write it down anyway. Circle the values and ideals that seem to you to be most important.

Thank you for playing. I understand that might have seemed a little silly. It *is* a little silly, but it's also important. Although, admittedly, unlikely to turn you into the world's first pirate prime minister, or whatever, it lets us harness the playful part of our mind; and *that* allows us to imagine more fully the kind of life we want. It's easy to know what you want when you're a kid, before you understand that the world is hard and sad and complicated – and exercises like this allow us the freedom to dream. How can we get what we want unless we know we want it? How can we know what we want unless we give ourselves the freedom to imagine it?

It's easy in our lives to lose touch with what we really wanted, just as it's easy to lose touch with who we are and where we are. The meditation exercises in the first chapter ground us; exercises like these release us from all the ties of daily life and allow us to ask ourselves (as we will on the next page) what we really want, and how far we have to go to achieve it.

Values Then, Values Now

Look at your words and doodles on page 68, in particular any of the values or ideals that you circled. Consider this question:

Do these values still matter to you now?

How have you integrated – or not integrated – those values into your adult life?

You don't need to write anything down in response to these questions, but I do want you to use the circled words to make a list on the next page: a list of five values that are important to you as you are now.

There's no judgement here, because nobody else will see this notebook. It's just for you, remember.

My Five Values

1. ....

2. ....

3. ....

4. ....

5. ....

Are you living up to these values?

....

....

Where in your life are you achieving these values, and where could you be better?

....

....

....

By being in touch with our core values, we can build a kind of mission statement for ourselves: a mission statement and a series of goals. Kaizen is a business-efficiency strategy at heart, and so we're going to use that to help us: we're going to build a mission statement and a five-year plan for ourselves as if we were a company trying to become the next big thing. We can't *standardize, measure, compare, innovate and standardize* unless and until we know what we're hoping to achieve by it.

Mission Statement and Goal Pyramid

Now, we're going to use these values to write a mission statement for ourselves. To be the best parent I can be, for example.

Or: I want to support myself in a career that I actively enjoy, not one that I resent.

Or: I want to make enough money so that I can travel anywhere I like.

Or: I want to work actively and directly to help others.

Now, on the same page, we're going to use this mission statement to build a tiered system of goals, like this:

5 Minutes

1 Hour

Today

This Week

This Month

This Year

Ten Years

Lifetime Goals

What do you really want from the next five minutes? What do you really want from the next year? What do you really want from life? What, ultimately, brings you joy and satisfaction?

These are big questions, but that's the only way to know how to change your life for the better: to know what you want, and why you want it. You have to check in with yourself (and regularly!) to know that what you're doing now is aligning with where you want to go.

You can see from the pyramid that our lifetime goals spin out from the next five minutes. If your goals for today won't ultimately lead to getting where you want to be – and being who you want to be – why are you attempting them? Everything you're doing should be leading up to those goals: the tiniest movement. Nothing should be random. Even your daily routine should be leading you somewhere useful. When you're doing anything, ask yourself: why? Why am I doing this? Five-why isn't just for when we have a problem: it can also be incredibly useful as a tool for analysing our ordinary lives too.

Timetable Two

Are you using every one of your hours well?

Let's look at the timetable of a typical day we made earlier (see page 65). Ring in red anything that's not helping you achieve your goals. (You're going to be ringing in red a *lot* of the time you earmarked for staring into space.) These red rings? These are the places where we're going to *innovate*. (Remember that? That's another one of the key pillars of kaizen.)

Draw up a new timetable – thinking about your mission statement and your goals for the next five minutes, the next week, the next year, for life – that works for you. Think logically: work backwards from your goals. Want to run a marathon? You need to train. Want to train? You need time to go to the gym. Need more time? You need to get up earlier. Need to get up earlier? You need to go to bed earlier. Want to go to bed earlier? You need to stop watching Netflix and turn your phone off. You get the idea, right?

Compare the two timetables. Here's the thing: I already know what you're going to find. You're going to find you've been wasting a lot of time. Don't worry. From now on, you're going to waste a lot less. Noticing a problem and making a change? That's half the secret, right there.

Make a list of the top five places you've been wasting time — and then think of five ways that you could make each place more efficient, and more in line with your goals.

(And if you're struggling with this? Help is in the next chapter . . .)

1. ....

2. ....

3. ....

4. ....

5. ....

5

The Best
It Can Be

Kaizen and the
Five-S System

You have, as the quote says, exactly the same number of hours in the day as Beyoncé and Barack Obama. You have the exact same amount of time as everyone else: it's what you do with it that counts.

Obama famously wore the same suit (in blue, grey or – notoriously – tan) every day of his presidency in order to 'pare back' unnecessary choices from his life. I'm not saying throw out your wardrobe, but it's worth asking yourself: what am I overcomplicating here? What choices am I giving myself that I really don't need to worry about? What small things could I standardize across the board that would free up time for other, better things?

What small efficiencies could give me the time to make the life I want? Could I make even the unavoidable tasks of life simpler and (even!) more enjoyable? Am I using every minute efficiently to achieve my goals? Is everything around me structured in such a way as to help me achieve my goals? Could my moments be better?

The Five-S System

In this chapter, we're going to explore a secondary organization system which runs in parallel with kaizen. It's also Japanese and used in many of the same factories – including our old friends at Toyota! It's called the Five-S system, and it's a very simple structure that we can apply to almost anything – from our environment to our email inbox.

It's going to free up time, and free up space, and let us be the kind of efficient, beautiful person we've always wanted to be. It's going to provide the framework for all the innovation – and a support system for the standardization – that's so integral to kaizen practise.

Just like with kaizen, it was initially developed in manufacturing – but can be immensely helpful in terms of decluttering and streamlining our lives too.

The idea is this: we pick something we want to organize. Maybe a workplace, maybe a desk, maybe an email inbox or a wardrobe or a kitchen. For the thing we want to organize, we run through five stages, each marked with a word beginning with S (helpfully, this is true in both English and Japanese). At each stage, we're going to ask ourselves three questions, and we're going to take action based on our answers to them. Ready? Let's go.

1 | Seiri: Sort

Should this be here?

Is this supposed to be here?

Is it helpful for this to be here?

The Best It Can Be

Think the first phase of Marie Kondo: do I need to keep this email? Do I need this paperwork? Do these tights have holes in? Is that an odd sock? Do I need fifteen pairs of trainers, or six boxes of Christmas ornaments? What do I need this room/inbox/desk to do, and is everything that's here helping me in that goal?

Keep it simple: the fewer things we have, the less likely we are to get distracted by looking at them or fiddling with them or organizing them. The fewer things we have, the less likely they are to get in our way. Grab your bin bags (or the digital equivalent). And, for goodness' sake, once you decide to get rid of something – do it now. Do it right away. *Do the thing.*

2 | Seiton: Set in Order

Is this the best place for this to live?

Is this the best way for it to be organized?

Is this the best place for this to be when I look
at the whole?

Here's where your kitchen organization comes in, if you're
still thinking about those Kilner jars from the introduction.

Could I store these grains and flours more efficiently?
Could I file this paperwork in a more intuitive way?
Could I find a wallet for my credit card, and a hook for
my keys?

This step is all about labelling, organizing and finding a home for things. Stationery people: step this way. This is your time to shine. Label-makers, files, folders: all of this will be really useful to you here. And those four colours of Post-its. Find homes for things that fit, and put them away when you see them. (Just like with kaizen, sometimes this feels too simple to write down – but if you do it, and do it religiously, it will change your life.)

3 | Seisō: Shine

Is it the best it can be?

Is it working?

Is every part of it clean?

In short: wash up as you go along. Throw things away when they break, or fix them. Pair your socks when they come out of the washing machine. Leave things tidier than when you found them. Put your necessary things away in the places you've organized for them.

Ideally, by this step, you'd be leaving the room/inbox/desk/ whatever so clean and tidy that a stranger could see where everything is and is supposed to be. Is it the nicest room/ inbox/desk/whatever it's possible to be? How could we make this a nicer environment? (Here's the place for those terrariums and rose gold bits, to go with your Kilner jars.) People flourish in beautiful spaces; you flourish in beautiful spaces. Give yourself a chance.

4 Seiketsu: Standardize (1)

Do you need any help?

Can anyone help?

Is everyone doing their bit?

Traditionally, this is the part where you make sure everyone involved in the process knows what's up: knows when it's their day to clean, their responsibility to take out the trash or delete unwanted social-media comments (or whatever it is). And maybe now is a good time for you to ask for help.

You're going to need the people around you to join in, after all. You've taken responsibility for yourself – your goals, your fears, your failures, your mission statement – and now it's time to get everyone else involved, too.

Why? Because it's impossible for you to keep this going by yourself. It's impossible for you to do this bit without cooperation from your colleagues, kids, housemates – whoever it is who shares your space with you. Make a chore list. Heck, you could even make a chore wheel. Explain the new system and explain why it works (although if you've done steps 1–3 right, it should feel fairly intuitive).

4   Seiketsu: Standardize (2)

Where else can I apply this system?

Can I use these techniques anywhere else?

Would this work for my desk/workplace/hobby/
mysterious other?

While this isn't the traditional spin on 'standardize', it felt like
a sensible place to bring this up: could you apply this to
other areas of your life?

Could you, say, aim to tackle one room a week with this technique? Could you try it with your workplace if you started out sorting a kitchen, or with your gym bag if you started out sorting your emails?

Just as we considered doing a five-step/five-minute/five-thing exercise on a regular basis, could you apply the five-S programme once every five days?

5   Shitsuke: Sustain

Why?

And why?

And are you sure?

It takes 66 days to form a habit. Or 21. Or 254. Researchers are, apparently, divided: nobody seems to know how long it takes before things are second nature. Me, I'm not sure it matters. I'm not sure it matters to us, because we have to keep living in the moment.

You'll notice that even when we've been looking at long-term goals, we've always come back to what we're doing right now, and what we're going to be doing in the immediate future. That's because it's the only thing we have control over, and kaizen is all about control.

It's overwhelming to wonder if we're going to be able to keep up new habits long-term; and it's overwhelming to think about our lives as one clean sweep of us 'doing it right' and 'being perfect' that begins today. If we spend too long dwelling on the future, the present slips away, and before you know it, nothing's been done. The next five minutes, though? You can manage that.

If the first half of the secret to success is simply noticing when something is wrong, and working to change it; the second half is just this: don't overthink it. All that you can do is do it right, right now, and hope it's enough. Are you being as kaizen as you can be?

Are you fixing things when they break, cleaning things when they get dirty and answering emails as they come in?

Are you asking yourself why you're doing things, and really listening to the answer? Are you checking in with yourself to make sure the thing you're doing feels right to you at the time you're doing it?

Are you doing the thing when it needs doing? Are you taking responsibility when you get things wrong, and doing your best to put them right? Are you doing your best all round?

Then you're doing all right. You're doing better than all right. You're doing brilliantly. You're doing the thing, and doing it to the best of your ability, and you're doing it right now.

And that, in the long run, is what matters. Nobody can build a perfect century, but anyone can build a perfect minute. Anyone — even you.

Especially you.

An Hachette UK Company
www.hachette.co.uk

First published in Great Britain in 2020 by Gaia Books,
an imprint of Octopus Publishing Group Ltd
Carmelite House
50 Victoria Embankment
London EC4Y 0DZ
www.octopusbooks.co.uk

Distributed in the US by Hachette Book Group,
1290 Avenue of the Americas, 4th and 5th Floors, New York, NY 10104

Distributed in Canada by Canadian Manda Group
664 Annette Street, Toronto, Ontario, Canada M6S 2C8

ISBN 978-1-85675-429-3

A CIP catalogue record for this book is available from the British Library.

Printed and bound in China.

10 8 6 4 2 1 3 5 7 9

Publishing Director Stephanie Jackson
Art Director Juliette Norsworthy
Senior Editor Alex Stetter
Design and illustrations Abi Read
Assistant Production Manager Allison Gonsalves